Homes

Rosie McCormick

A+

First published by Hodder Wayland
338 Euston Road, London NW1 3BH, United Kingdom
Hodder Wayland is an imprint of Hodder Children's
Books, a division of Hodder Headline Limited.

This edition published under license from Hodder
Children's Books. All rights reserved.
Text copyright © Rosie McCormick 2003

Design: Perry Tate Design, Language consultant: Andrew Burrell,
Consultant: John Lace

Published in the United States by Smart Apple Media
1980 Lookout Drive, North Mankato, MN 56003

Library of Congress Cataloging-in-Publication Data

McCormick, Rosie.
Homes / by Rosie McCormick. p. cm. — (Starters)
Summary: Photographs and easy-to-read text introduce many different kinds of
places that people around the world call home.
Contents: What is a home? — Homes made of wood — Homes made of mud —
Leaves, reeds, and even stilts — Rocks and caves — Mobile homes — Unusual homes
— Glass, brick, and steel — Homeless — Communities.
ISBN 1-58340-261-6 1. Dwellings—Juvenile literature. [1. Dwellings.] I. Title. II. Series.
TH4811.5.M39 2003 392.3'6—dc21   2003042414

9 8 7 6 5 4 3 2 1

The publishers would like to thank the following for permission to reproduce
photographs in this book: Robert Harding; 5 (top) / Impact; cover, 6, 9, 15, 21-22 /
Corbis; 5 (bottom), title page, 7, 10, 13-14, 16-17, 20, 24 (fourth from top) / Britstock;
8 / Eye Ubiquitous; 11 (bottom), 12, 19 (top), 24 (top and bottom) / Still Pictures; 4,
11 (top), 24 (third from top) / James Davis Travel Photography; 18, 19 (bottom), 24
(second from top) / Science Photo Library; 23

Contents

What is a home?

The place where we live, eat, sleep, and play is called our home. There are many different kinds of homes.

Sometimes natural materials such as wood, stone, or mud are used to build homes. Man-made materials such as bricks, concrete, or glass are used, too.

Tree houses keep people safe from dangerous animals.

Igloos are made
of frozen snow.

Cottages are
built to last a
very long
time.

Homes made of wood

In many parts of the world, wood is used to build homes. Wood is a strong material and is easy to build with. Wooden houses are good at keeping heat inside.

In northern countries, many wooden houses have sloping roofs so winter snow can slide off.

In Russia, wooden summerhouses are beautifully decorated.

In the Dominican Republic, people paint their wooden houses in bright colors.

7

Homes made of mud

In hot, dry countries, people make mud bricks. The sun bakes the mud hard. Sun-dried bricks can last for hundreds of years.

Mud is easy to find, so there is plenty to use.

In Rwanda, Africa, people live in round houses made of poles, twigs, and mud.

The thick, mud-brick walls help to keep the house cool.

People who live in countries where there is a lot of water, such as Indonesia and Malaysia, live in houses on stilts.

Stilt homes keep water, snakes, and other creatures out.

Some people live in homes made of huge leaves found nearby.

These homes sit on giant reed mats that can float!

Rocks and caves

For thousands of years, people have made homes in caves and rocky places. Caves provide good shelter from the hot sun and cold winds.

In Spain, some people have made homes out of caves in the hills.

In the Australian desert, it's so hot that some people live in underground homes called dugouts.

These large rock towers in Turkey have been turned into homes.

13

Mobile homes

Some mobile homes, such as covered wagons and boats, carry people about. Others, such as tents, are carried by people.

In Mongolia, people often move their animals to new feeding areas. So they move their homes, too.

Some people live in boats.

In Asia, lots of people live in houseboats. They cook, eat, sleep, and even work on the boats.

Unusual homes

Sometimes people build houses that look a little strange! Would you like to live in one of these houses?

This houseboat in North America is very unusual!

The walls of this house in New Mexico are made out of old tires.

This house is made of mud and tin cans.

Glass, brick, and steel

Today, many people live in homes made of brick, concrete, glass, and steel. In big cities, many people live in homes built on top of each other. These are called apartments.

In Europe, North America, and Australia, most people live in homes built for just one family.

Long ago, kings and queens lived in grand castles built of brick and stone.

Homeless

People who are homeless have nowhere to live. There are millions of homeless people in the world today.

Many homeless people are refugees. Often, refugees do not have homes because of earthquakes, floods, or war.

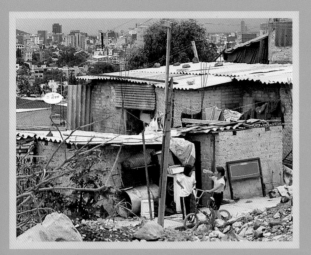

Homeless people are often poor and cannot afford a proper home.

Some homeless people live in cardboard boxes on the streets.

Communities

Most people are part of a community that they also call home. A community is made up of people living and working together. Villages, towns, and cities are communities.

People often work together to keep their communities safe, clean, and happy.

Although people live in different places and in different ways, all of us live on Planet Earth. We must all take good care of this special home.

Glossary and index

Brick A block of clay hardened by fire or the sun. **18-19**

Community People living together in the same place. **22**

Concrete A mixture of cement, water, sand, and gravel that hardens as it dries. **18**

Glass A hard, see-through material that can break quite easily. **18**

Man-made Something made by people. **4**

Mobile Something that is easy to move. **14**

Mud Wet earth that can be molded and becomes hard when it dries. **4, 8**

Reed A tall, strong grass that grows in places that are wet. **10-11**

Steel A type of metal that is very hard and strong. **18**